I0409362

Embrace the beauty of pregnancy with this soothing coloring book. Let your creativity flow as you relax and unwind during this special journey.

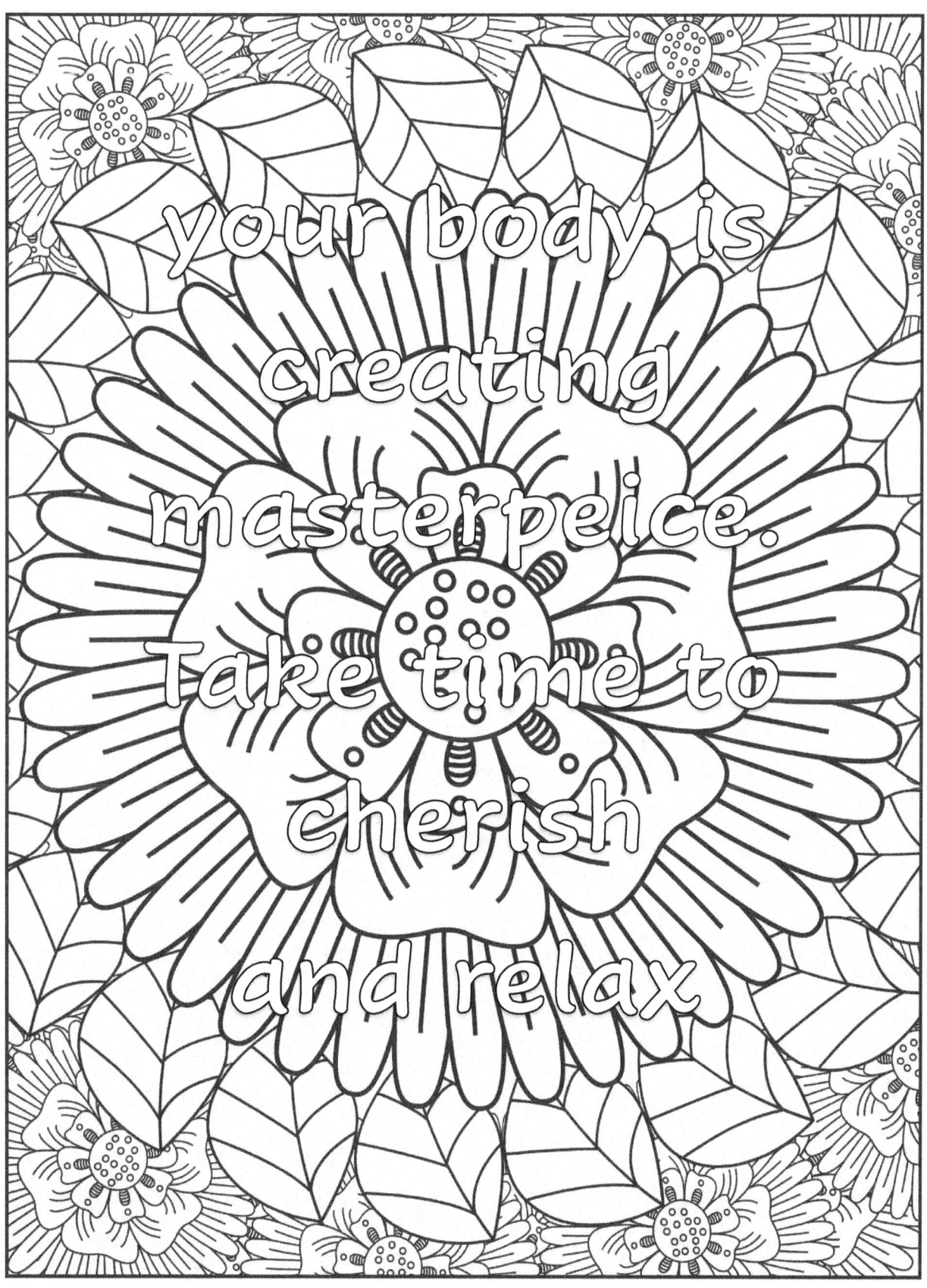

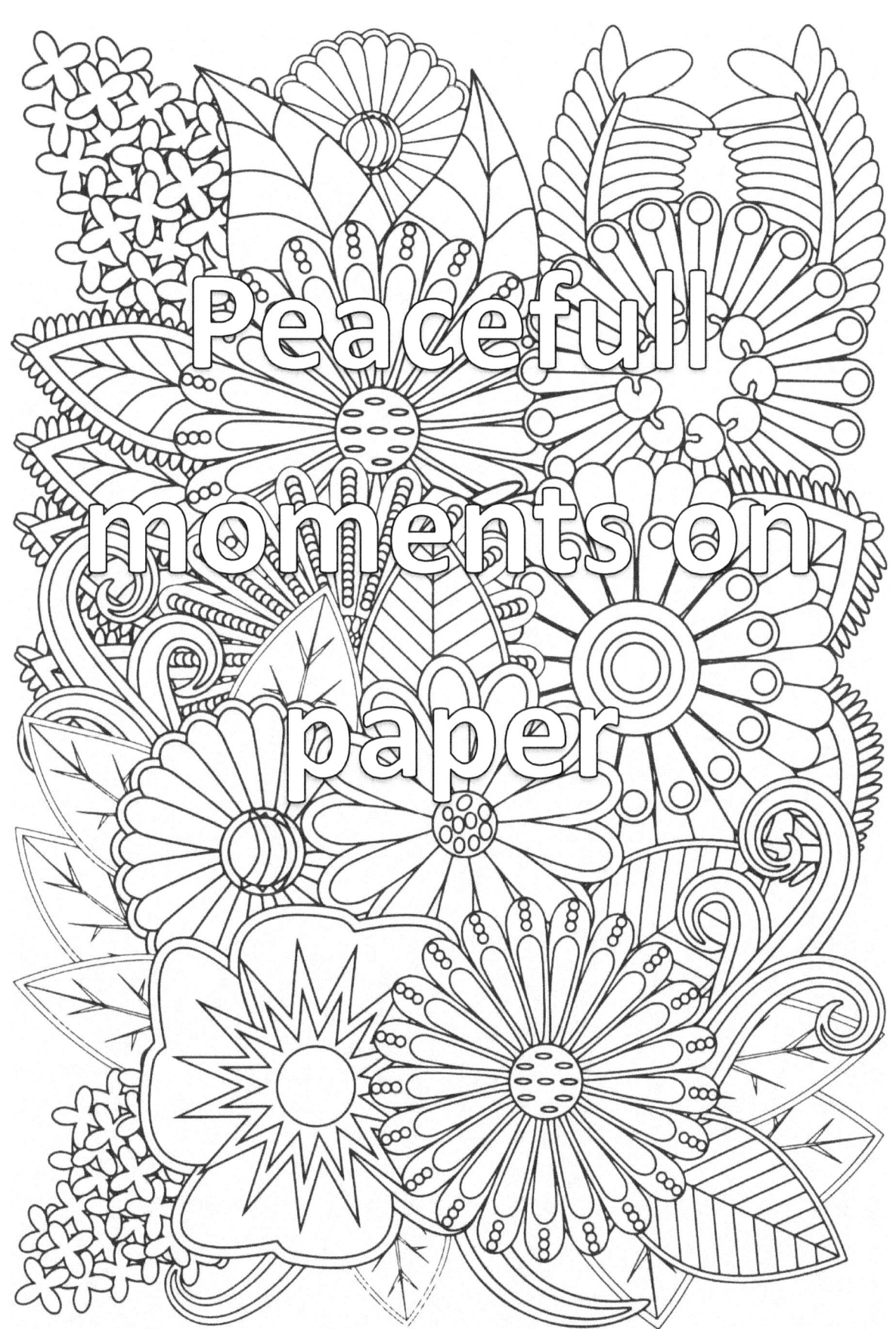

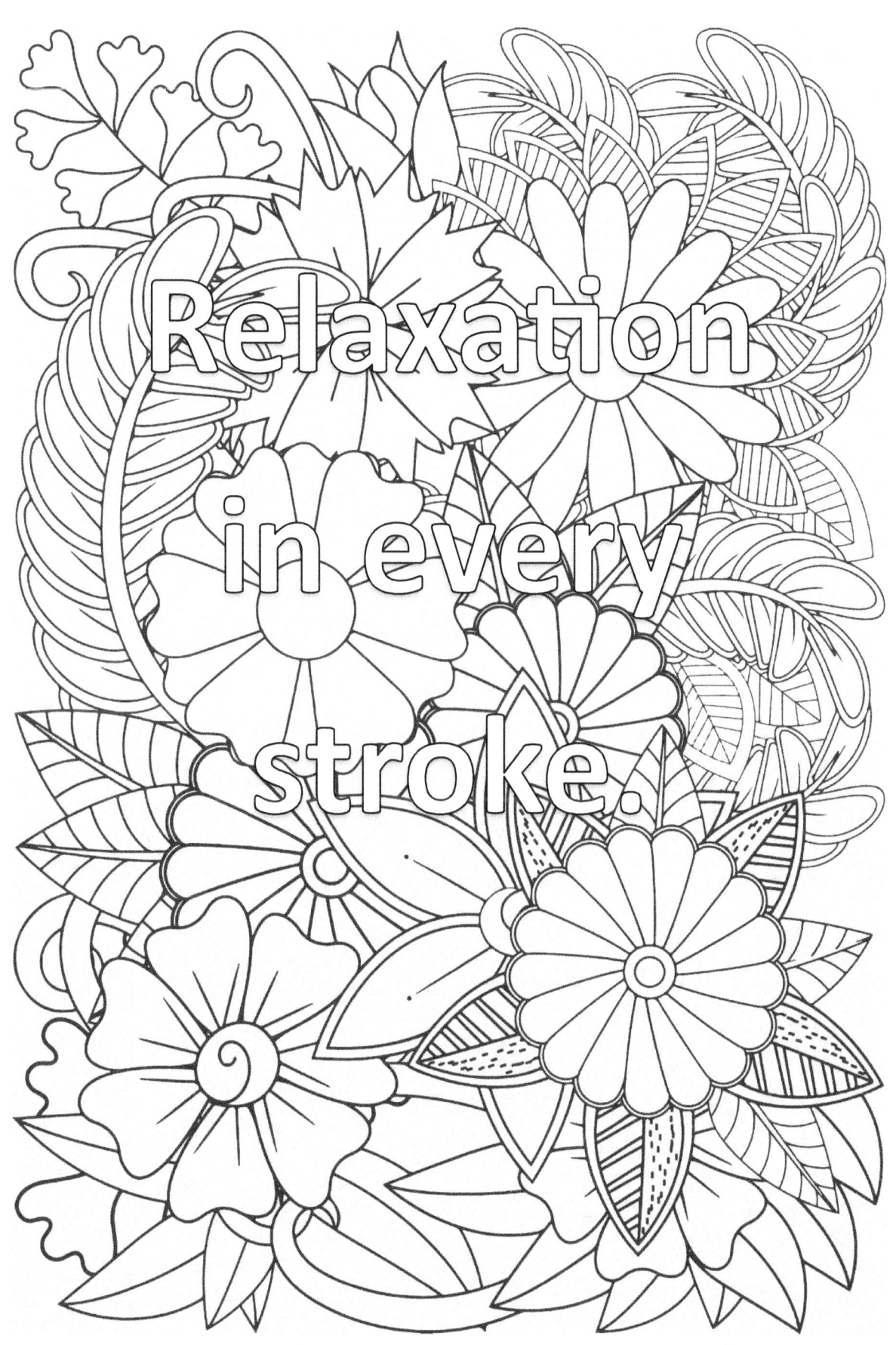

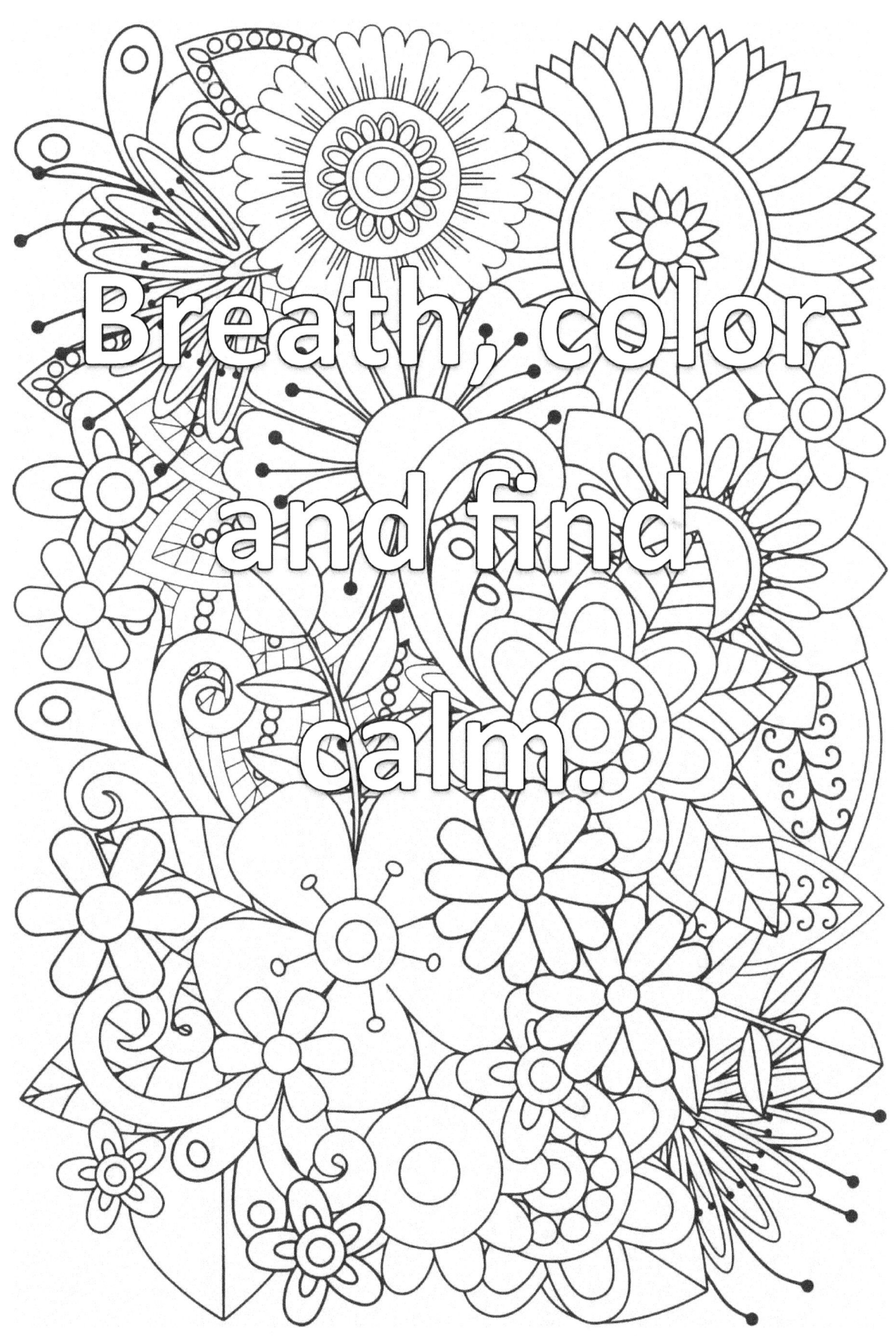

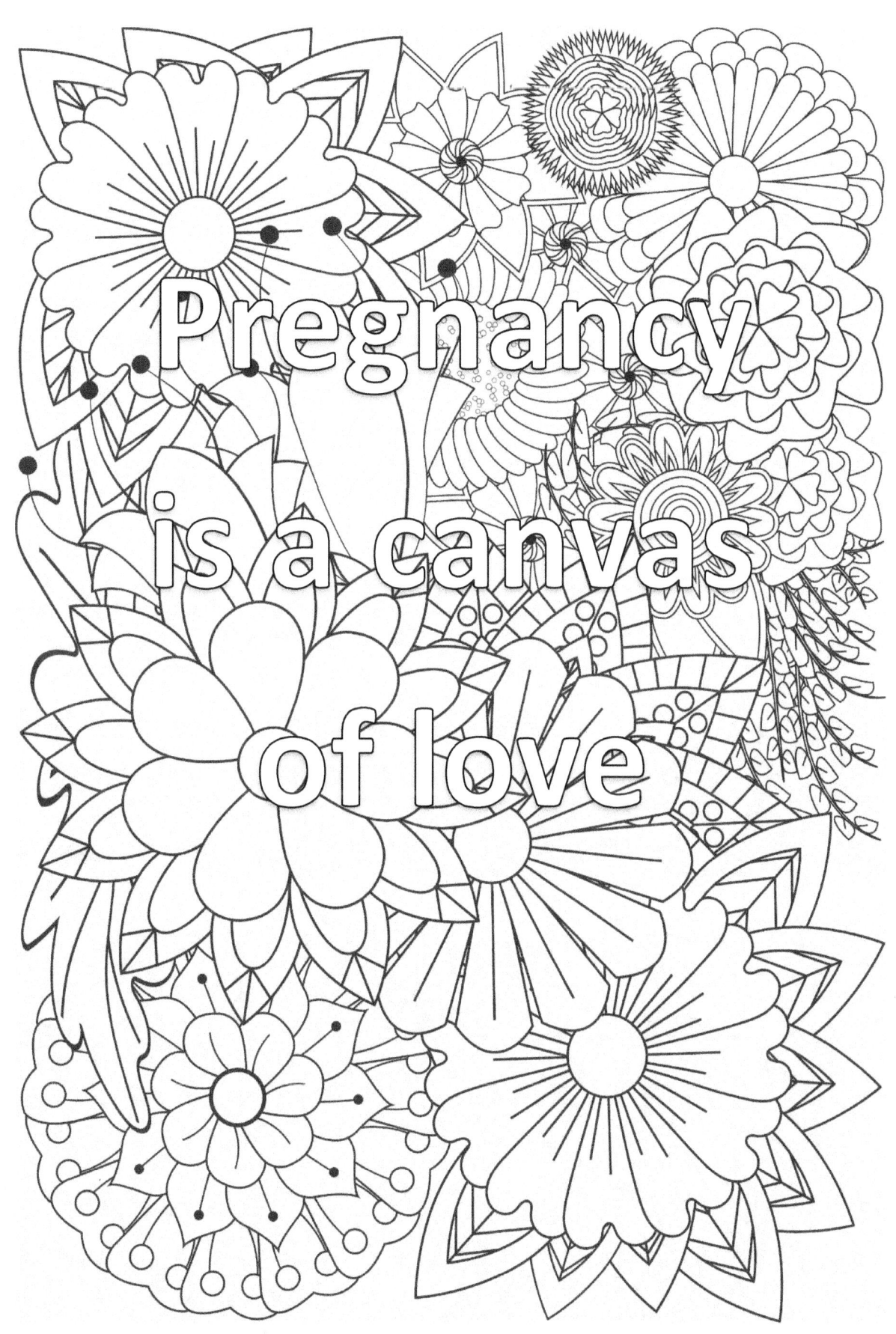

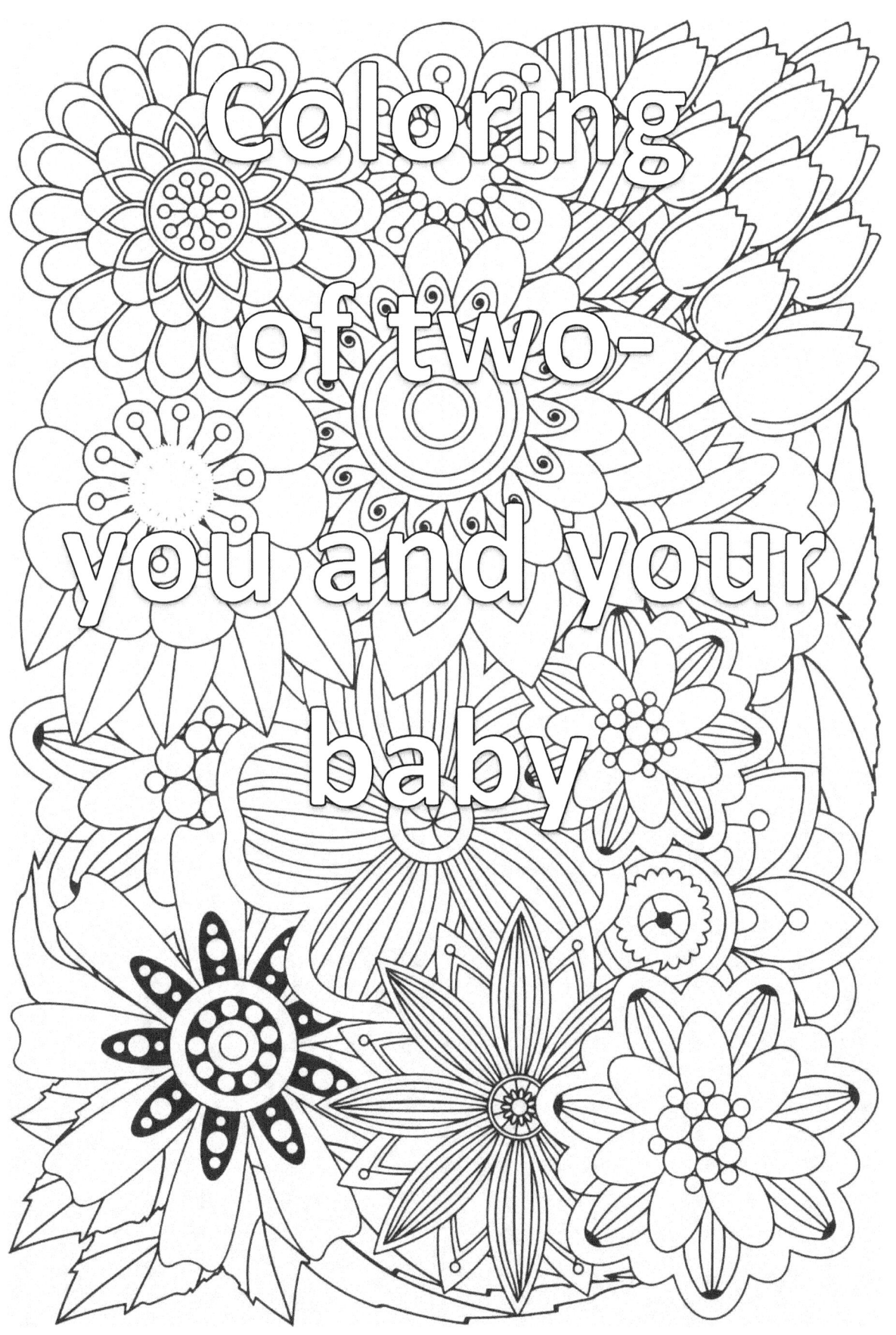

Coloring of two-you and your baby

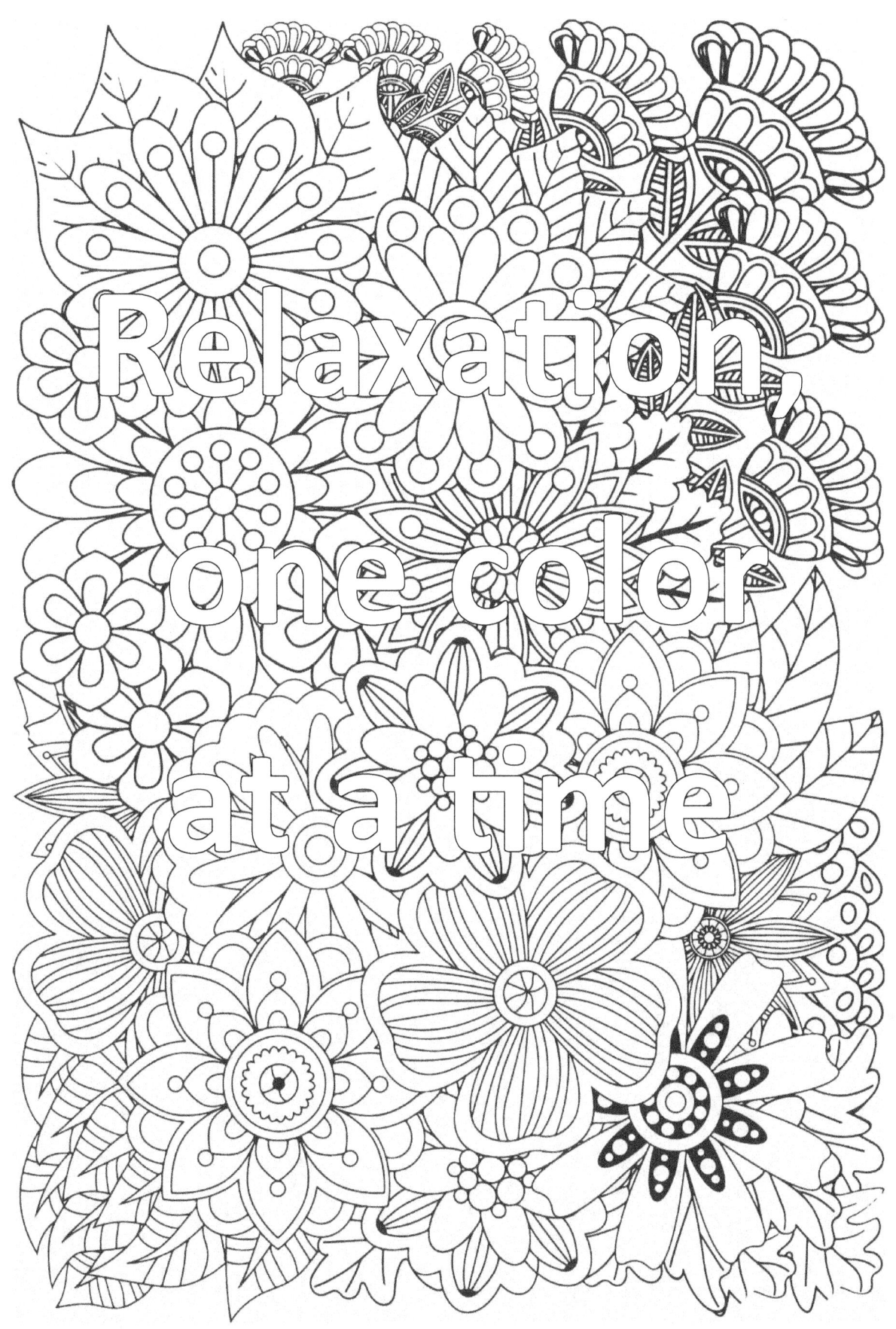

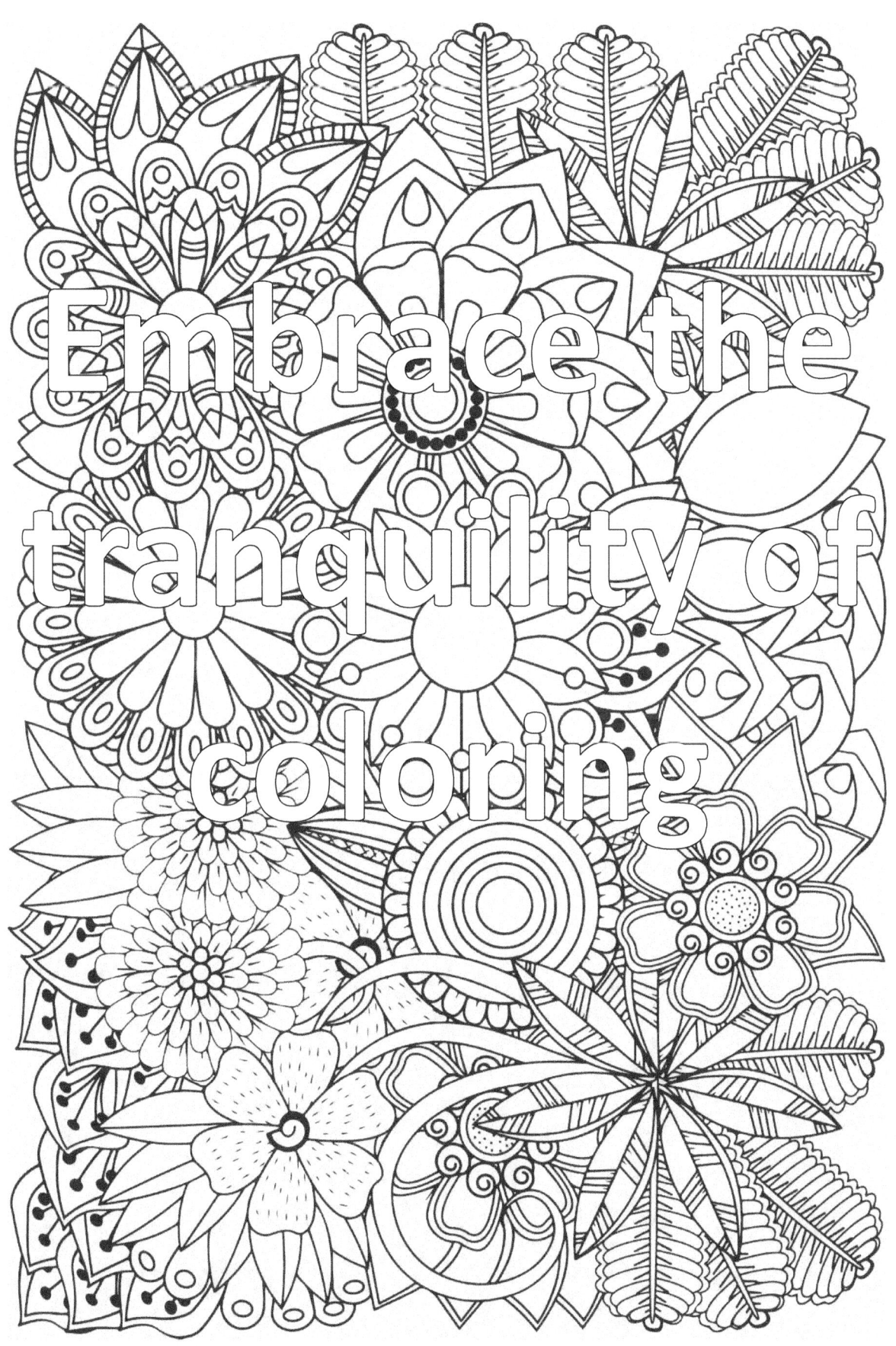

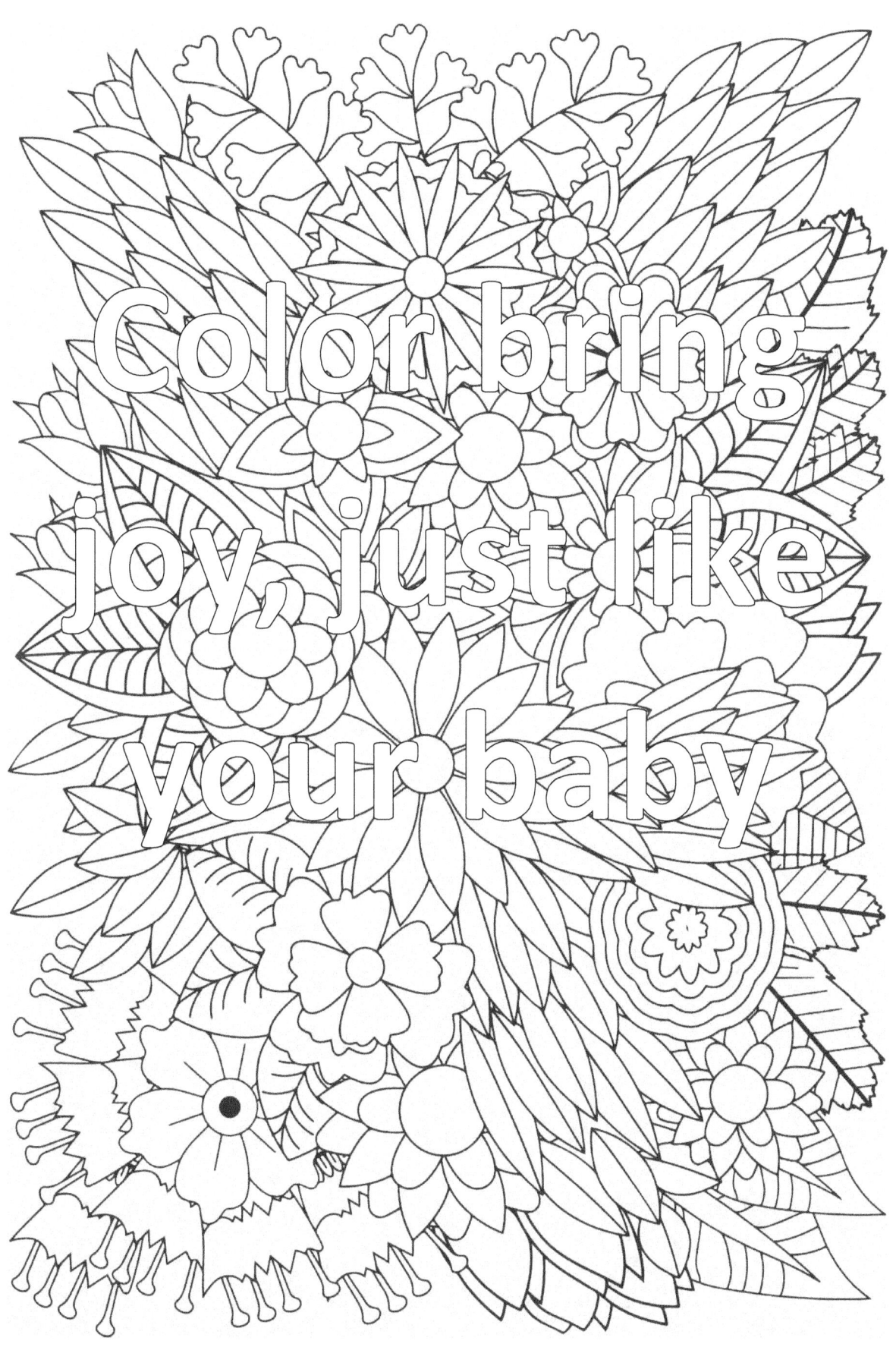

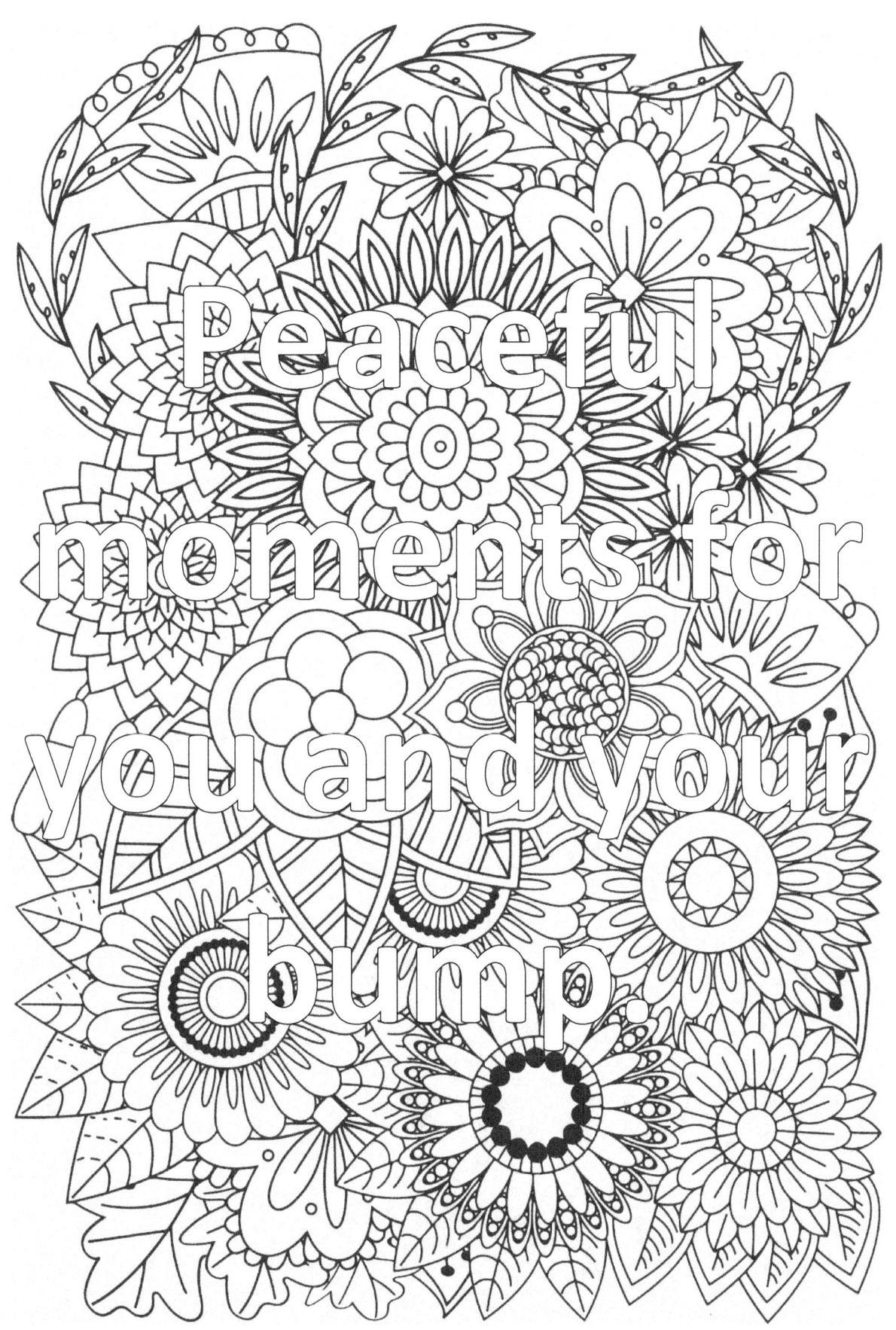

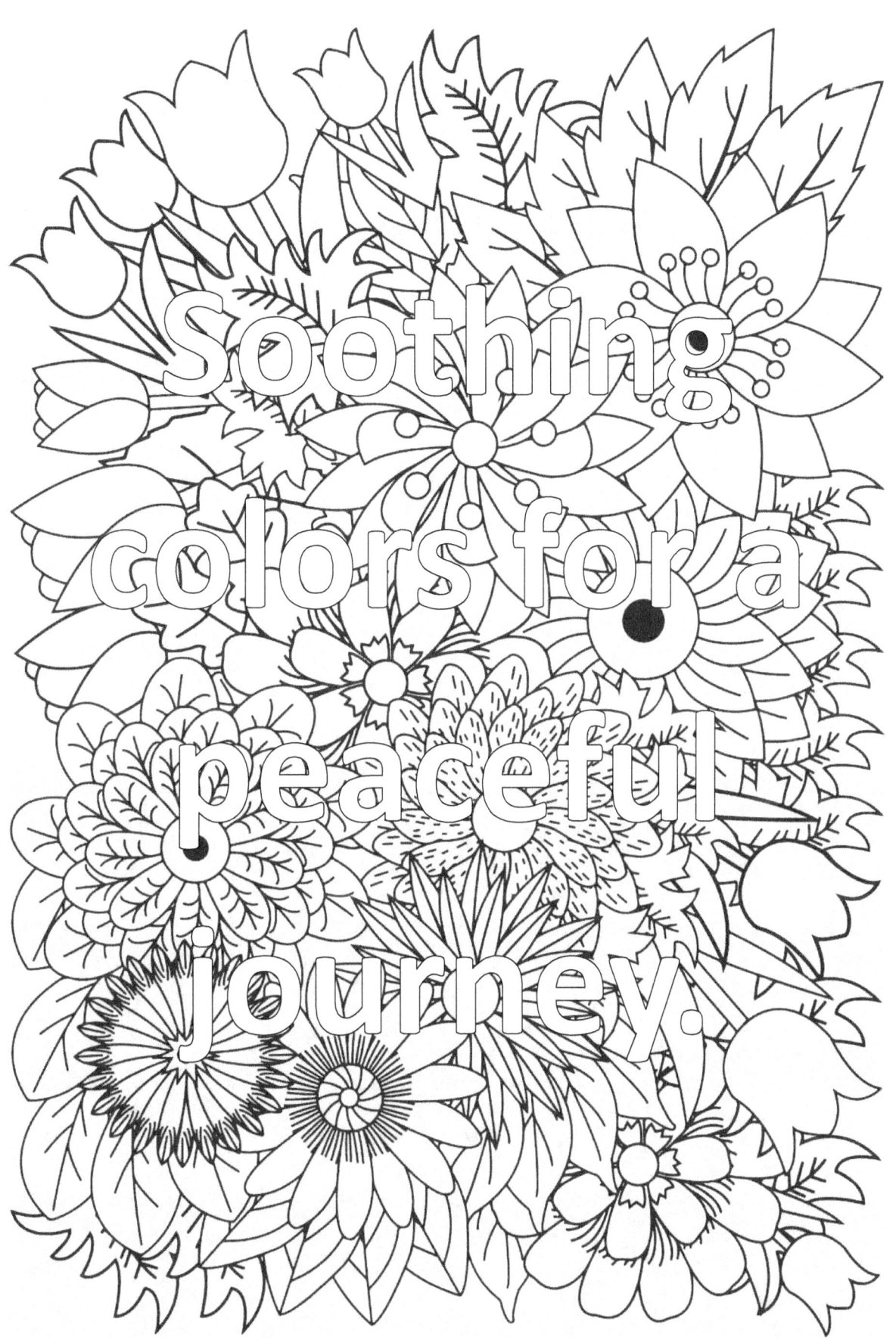

www.ingramcontent.com/pod-product-compliance
Lightning Source LLC
Chambersburg PA
CBHW082207290526
45794CB00008B/3460